This notebook belongs to:

_____

_____

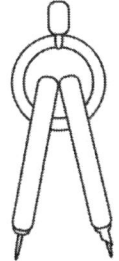

Please leave a review because we would love to hear your feedback, opinions, and advice to create better notebooks and material for you. Thank you so much.

You are awesome!

MATHEMATICAL MATRIX

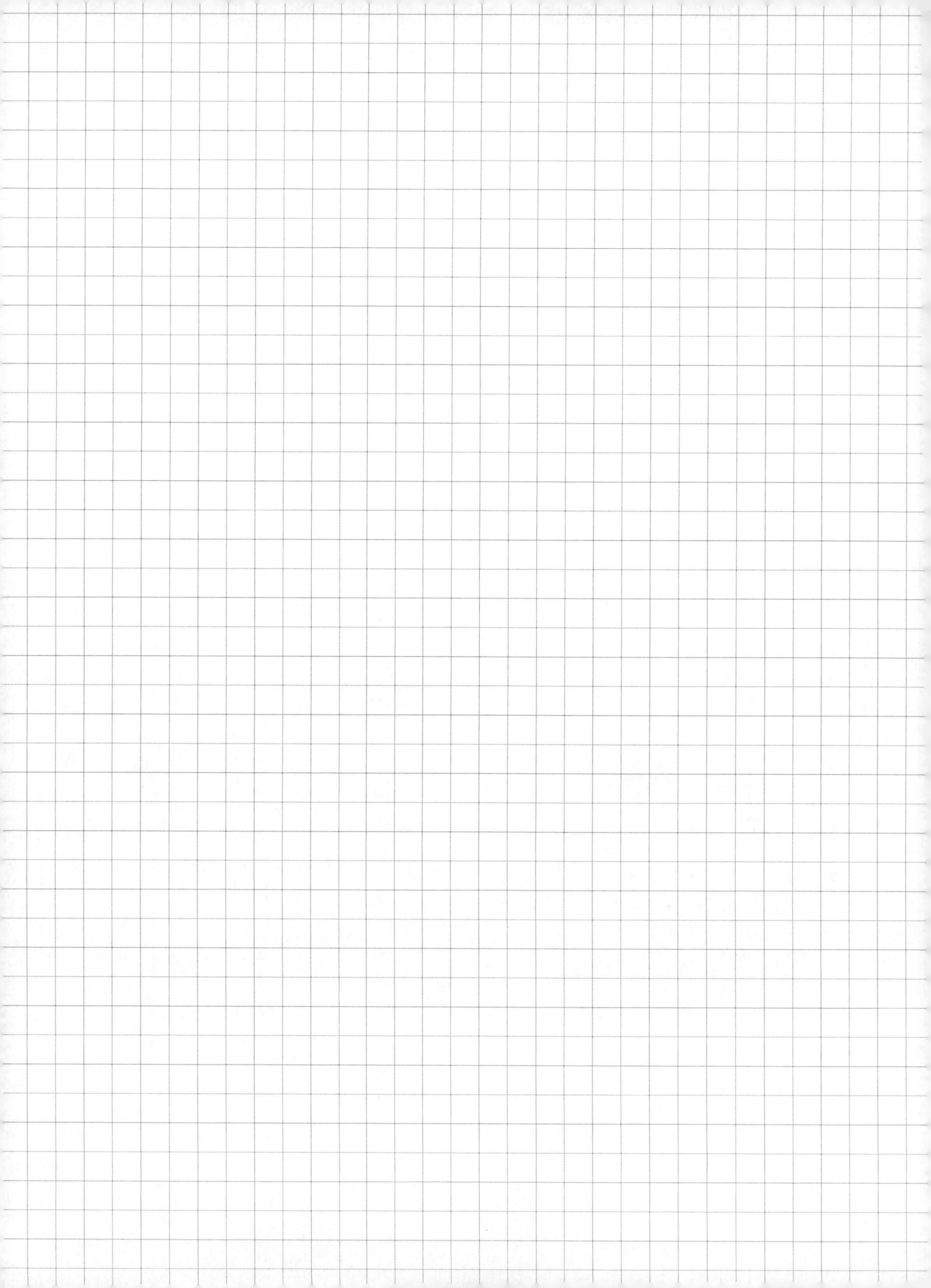

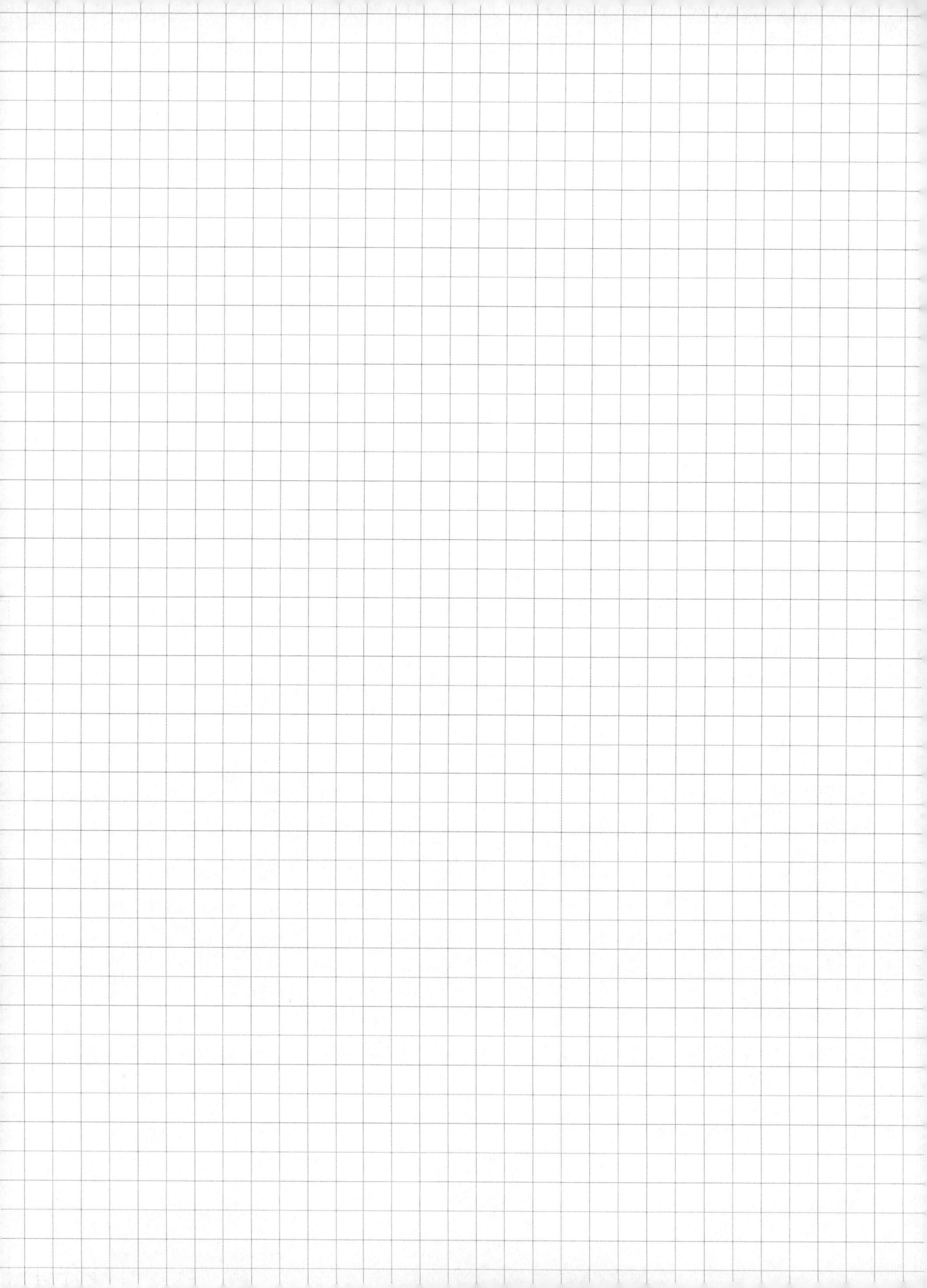

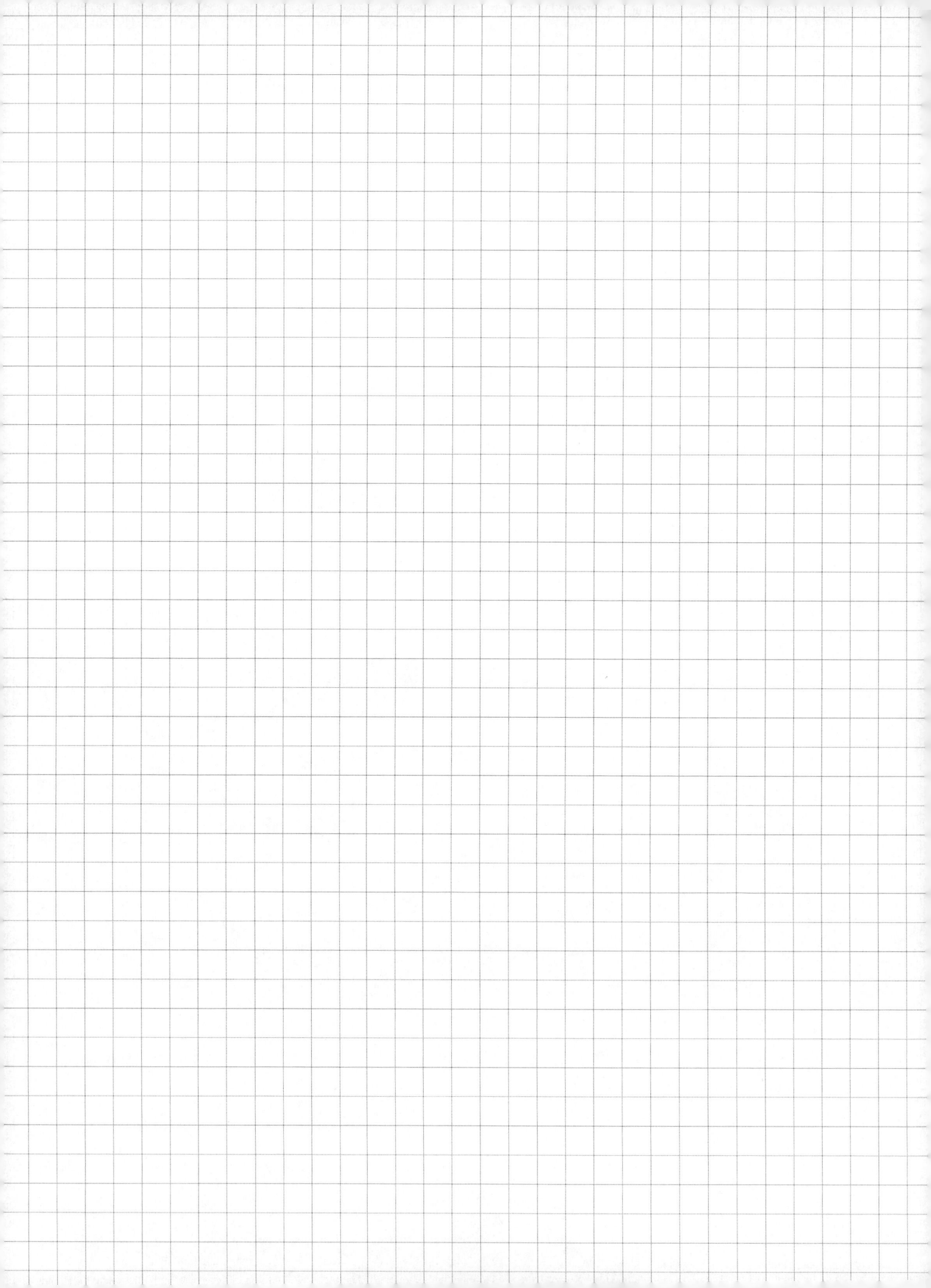

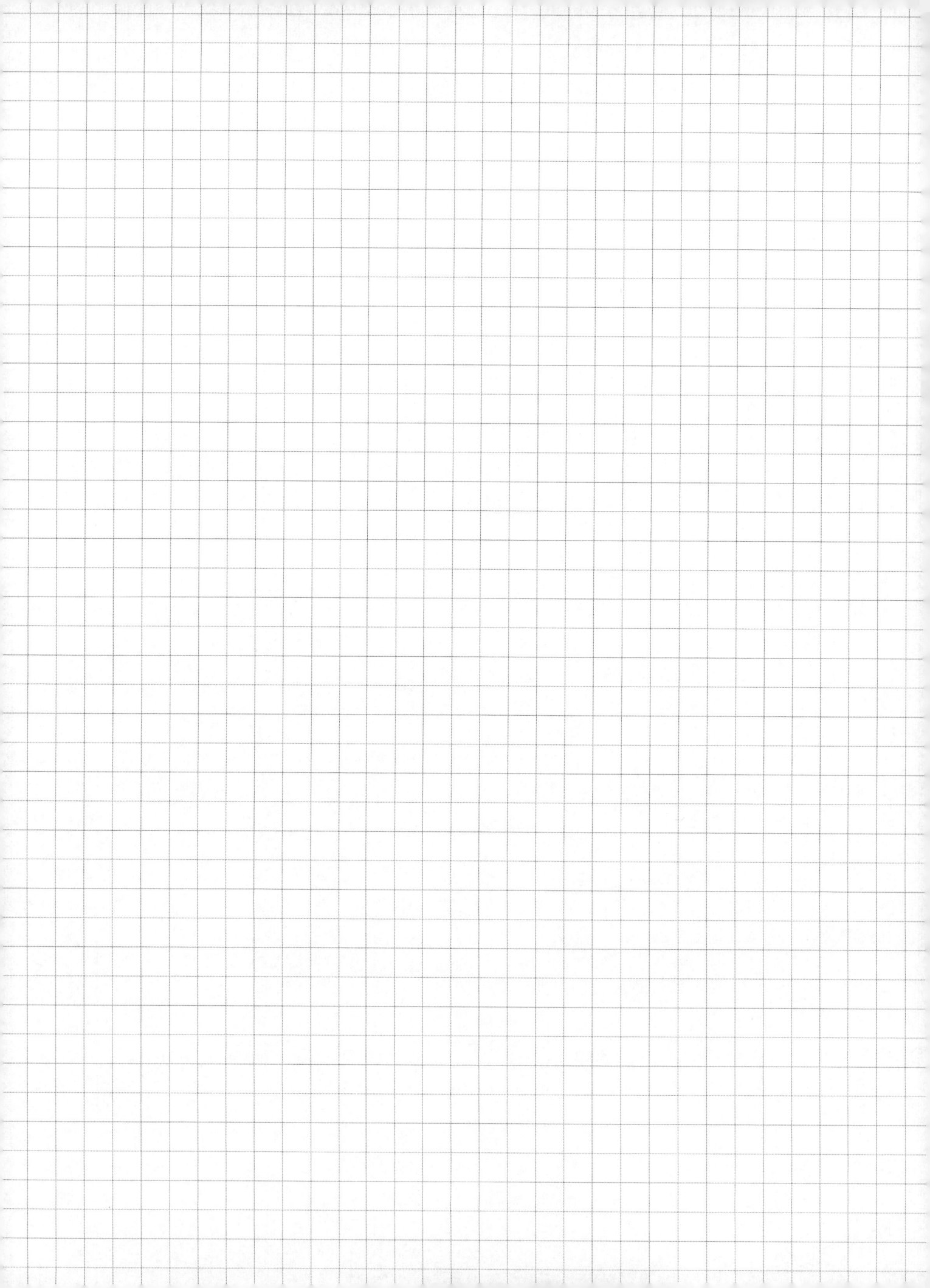

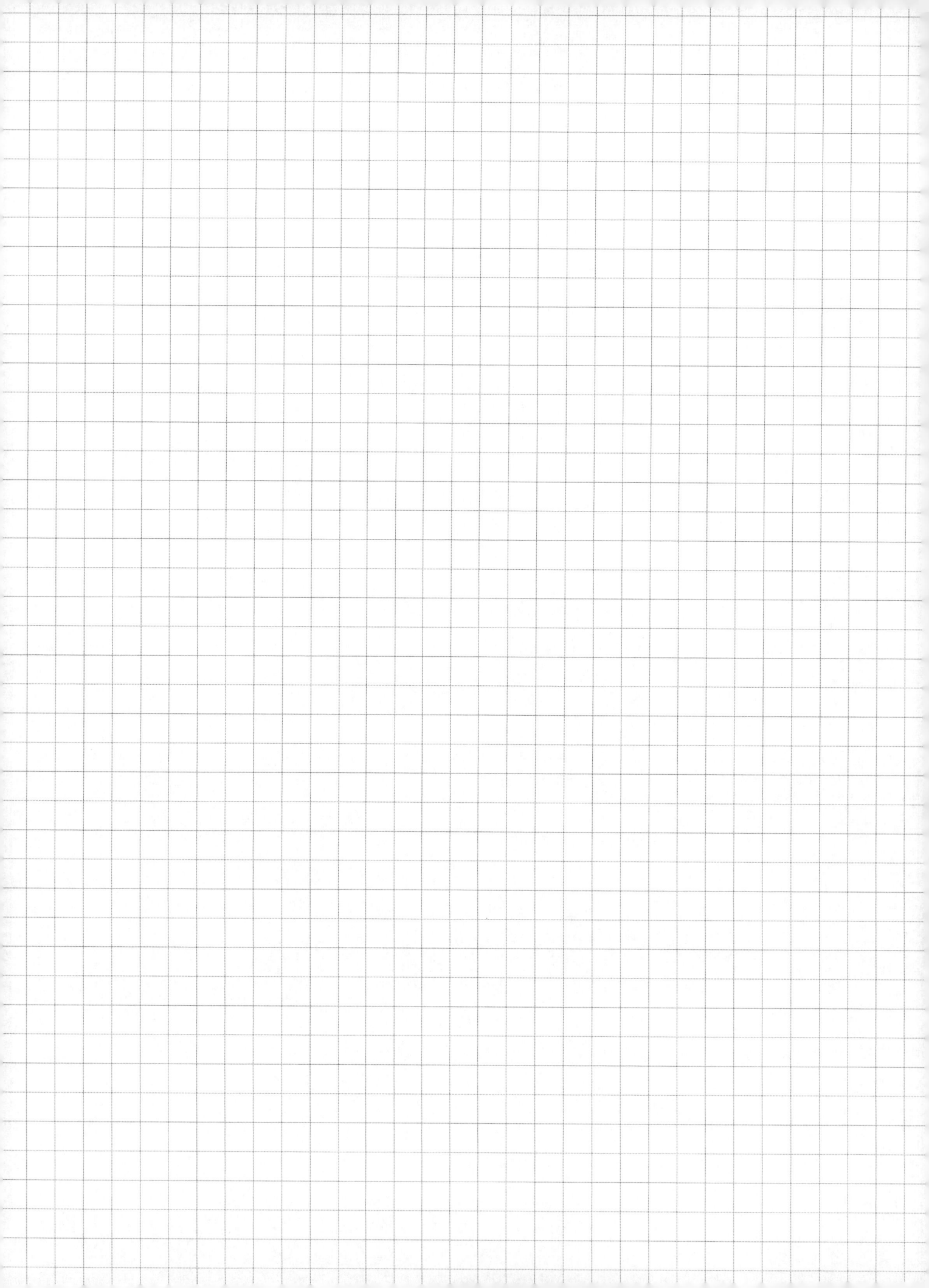

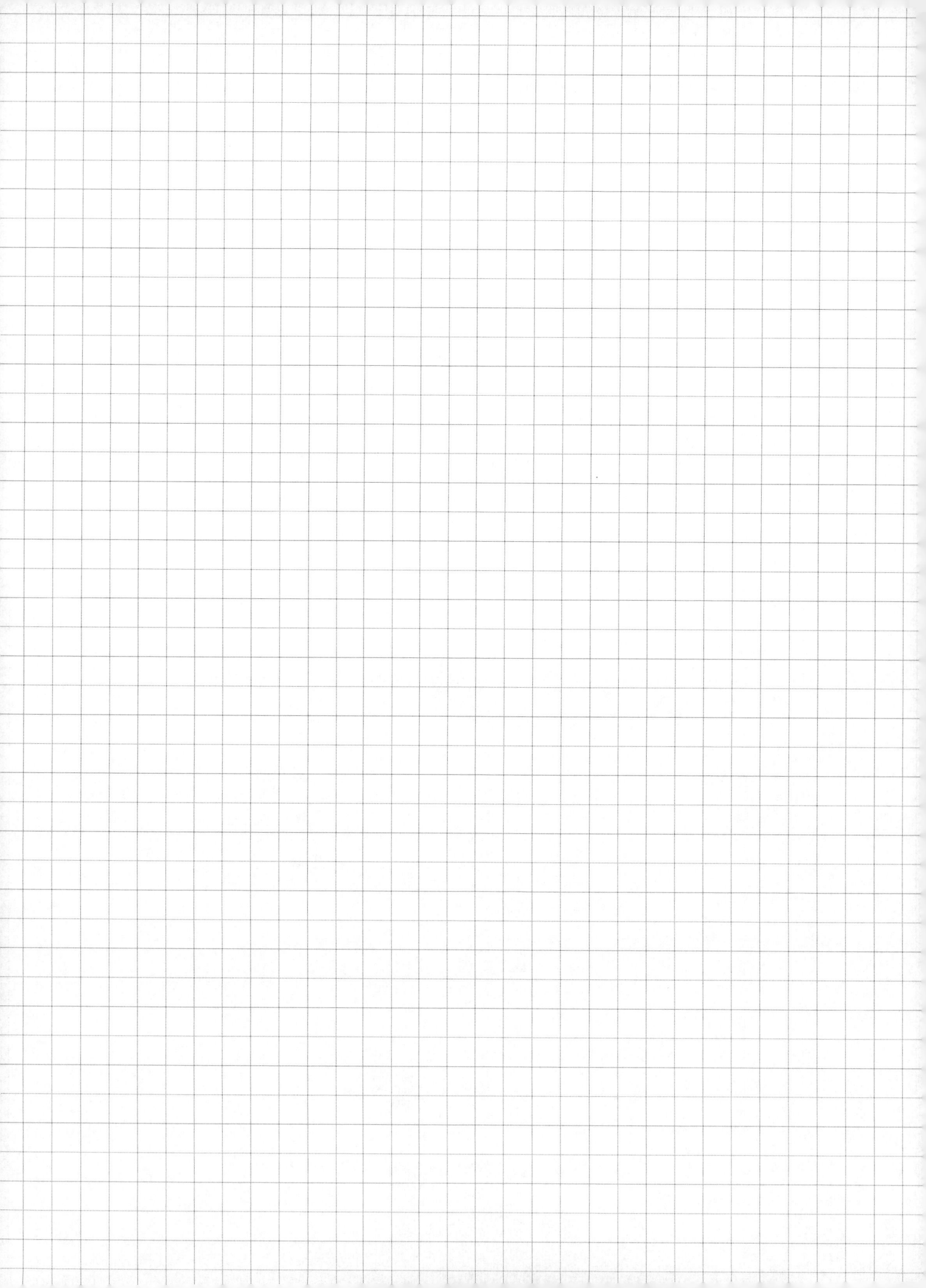

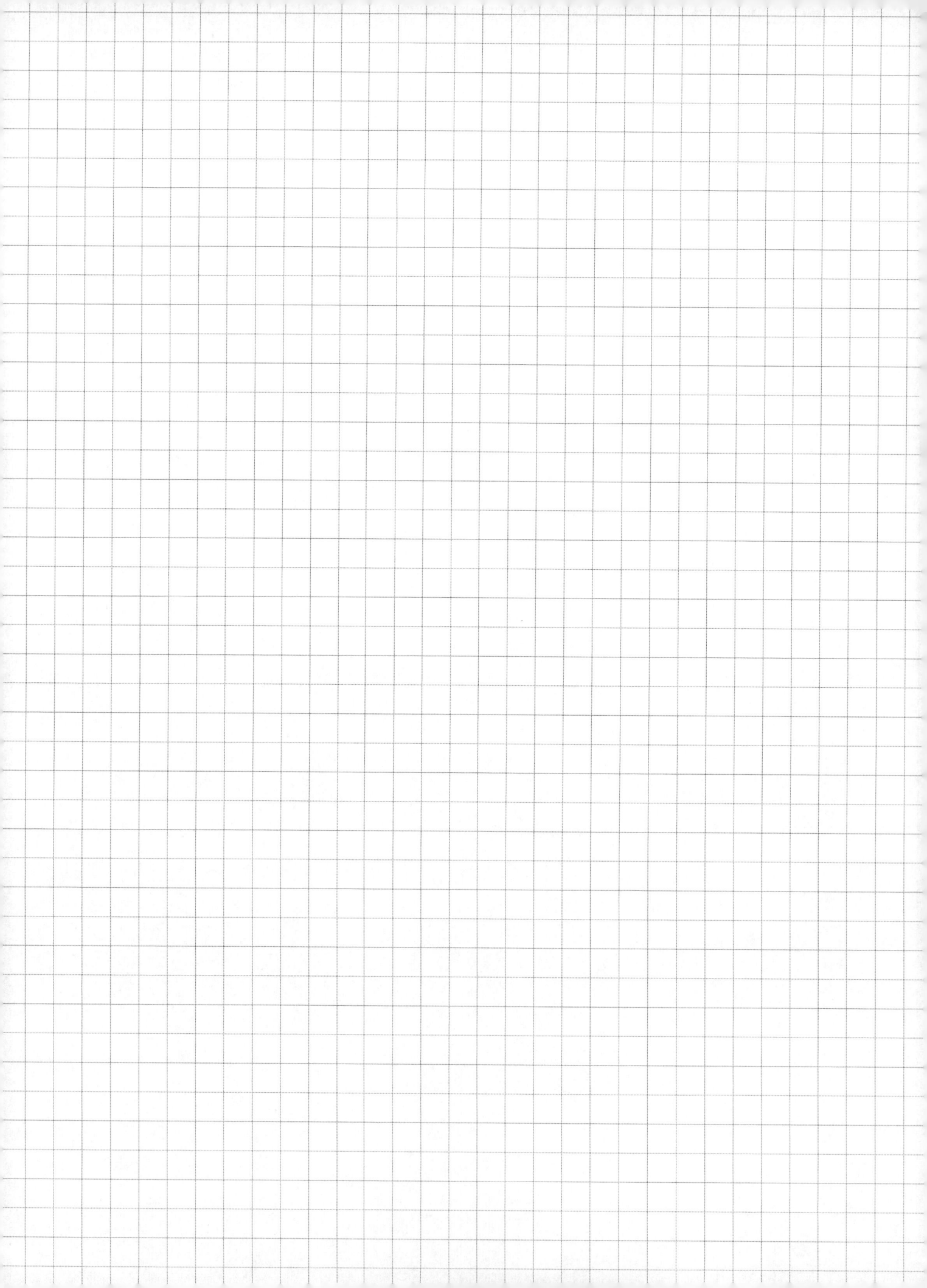

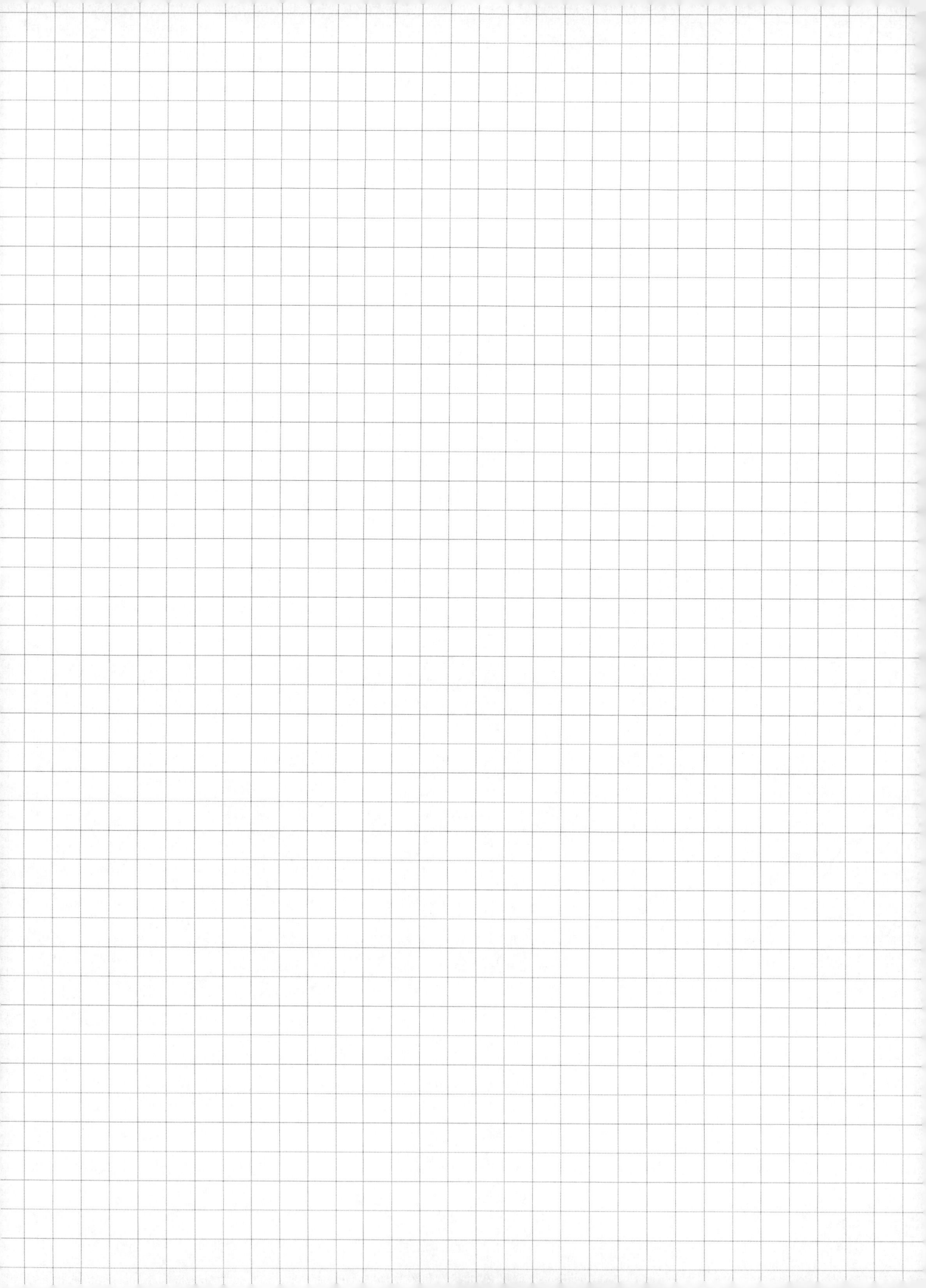

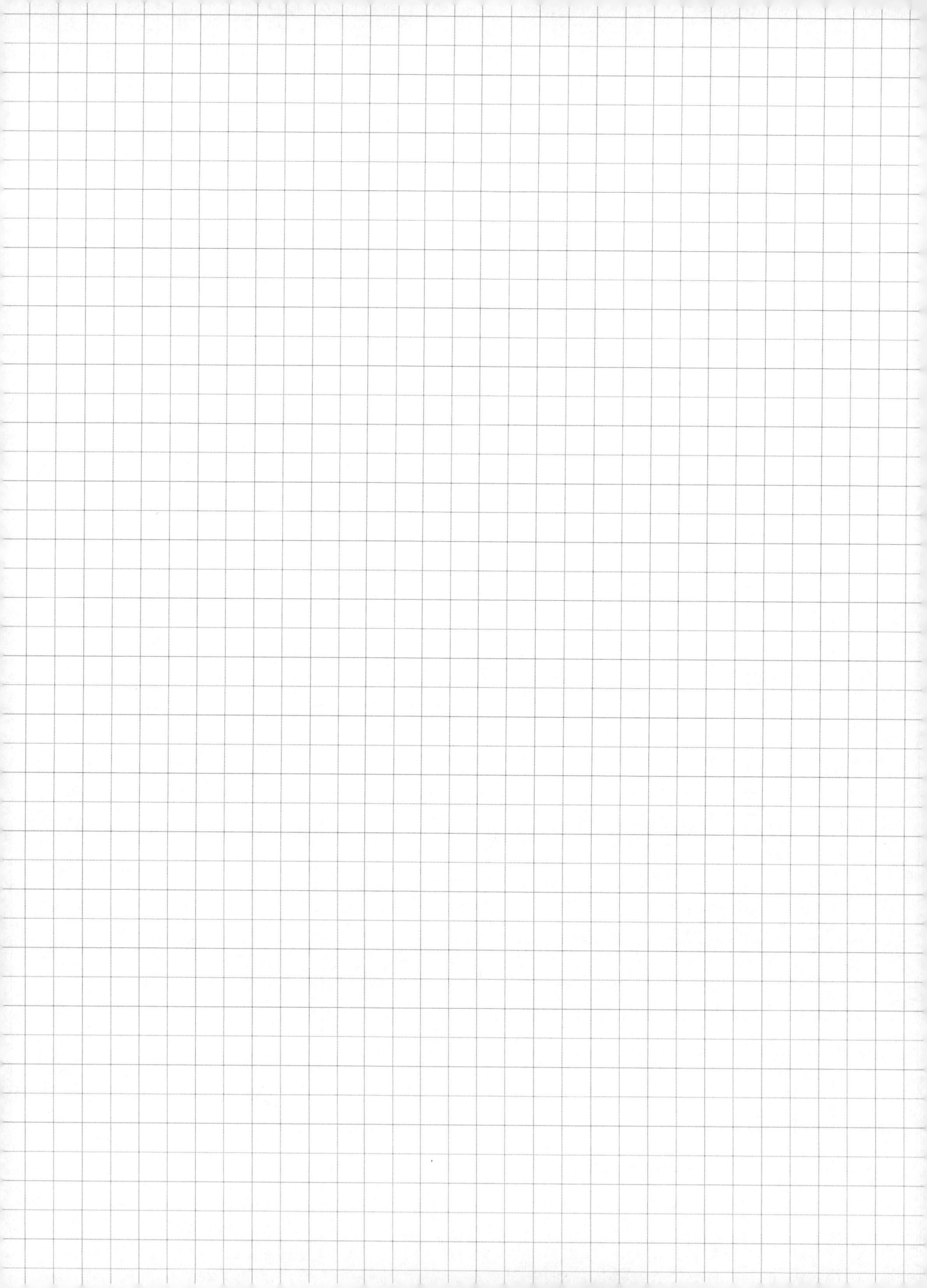

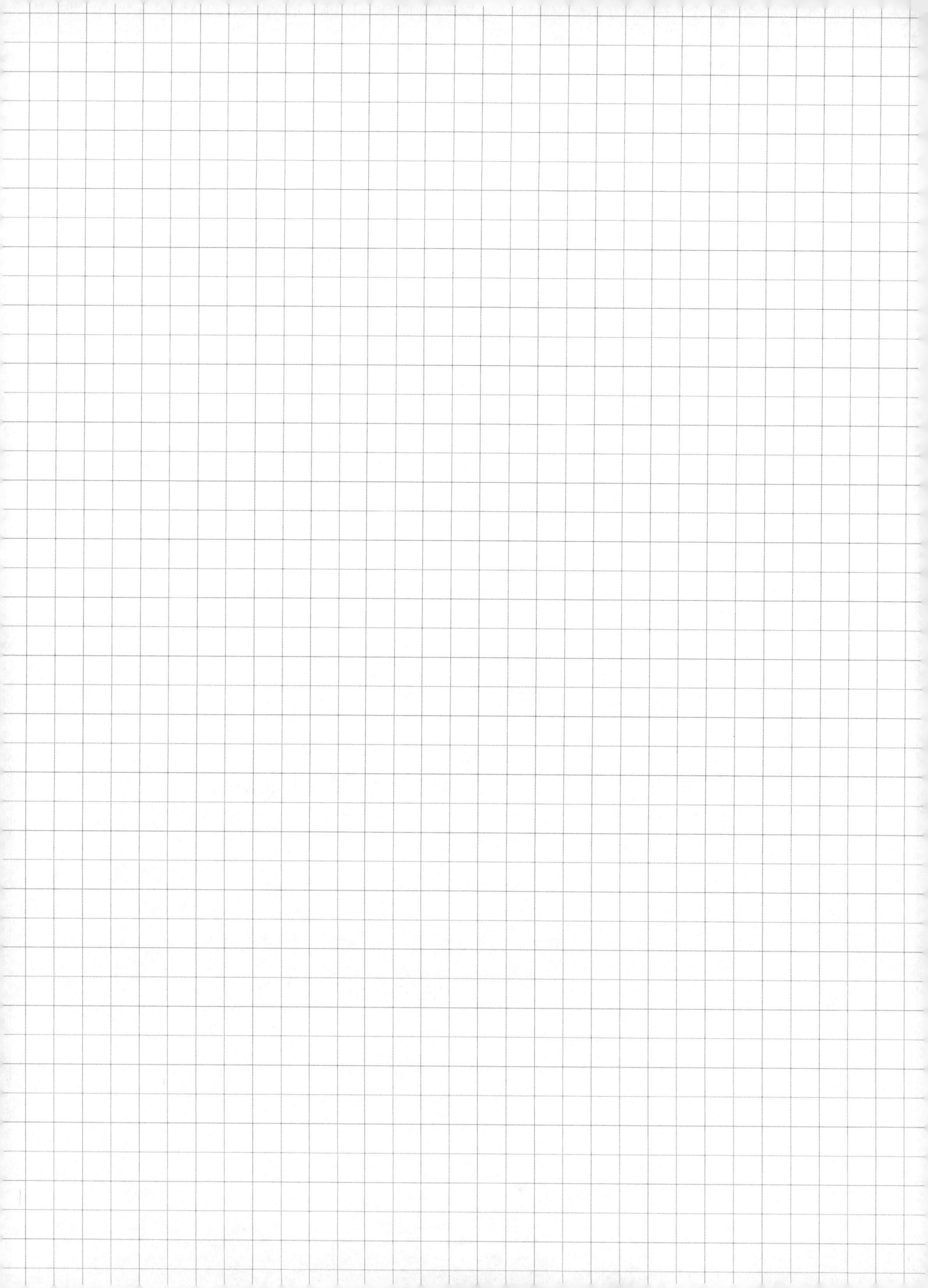

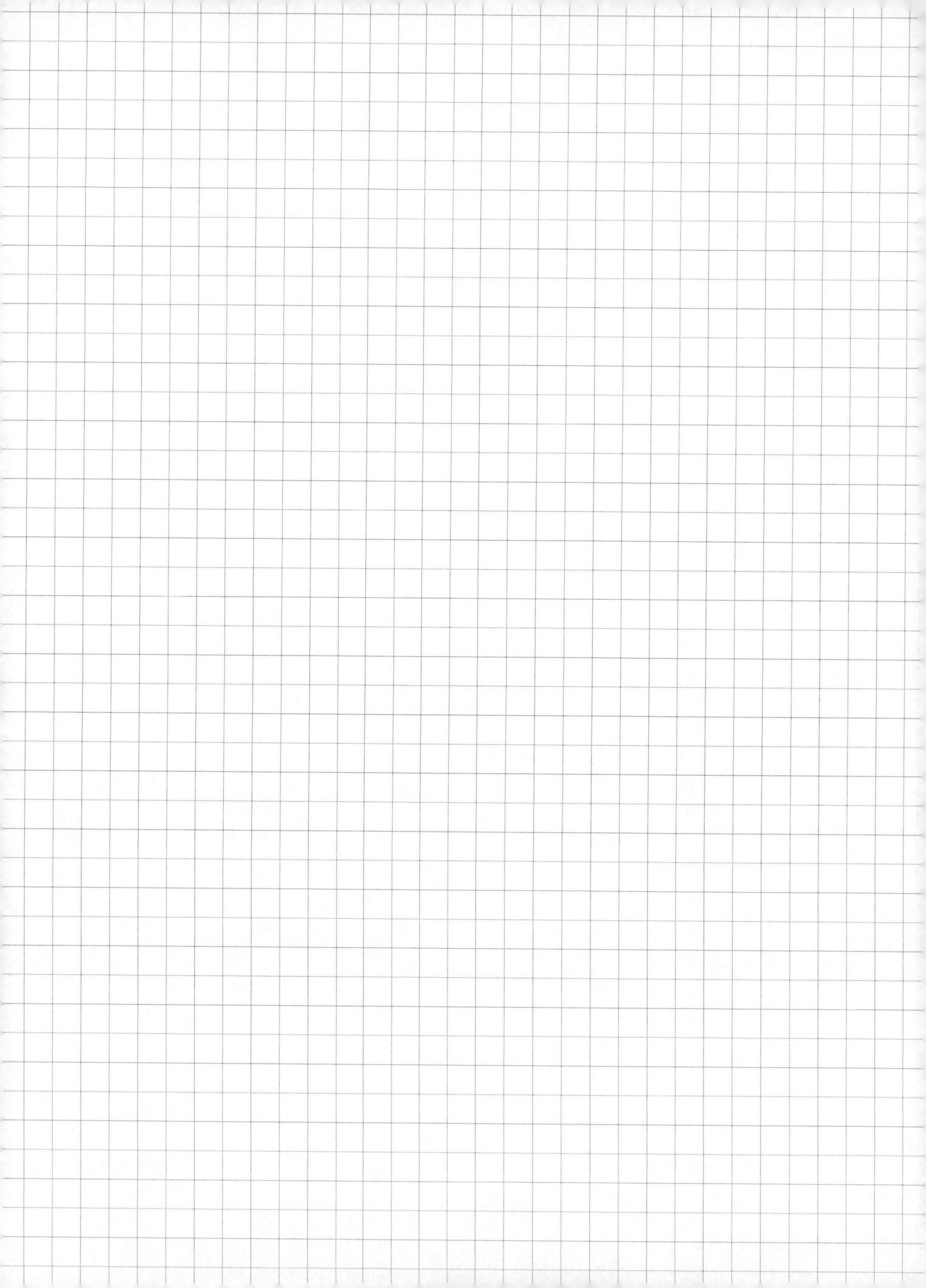

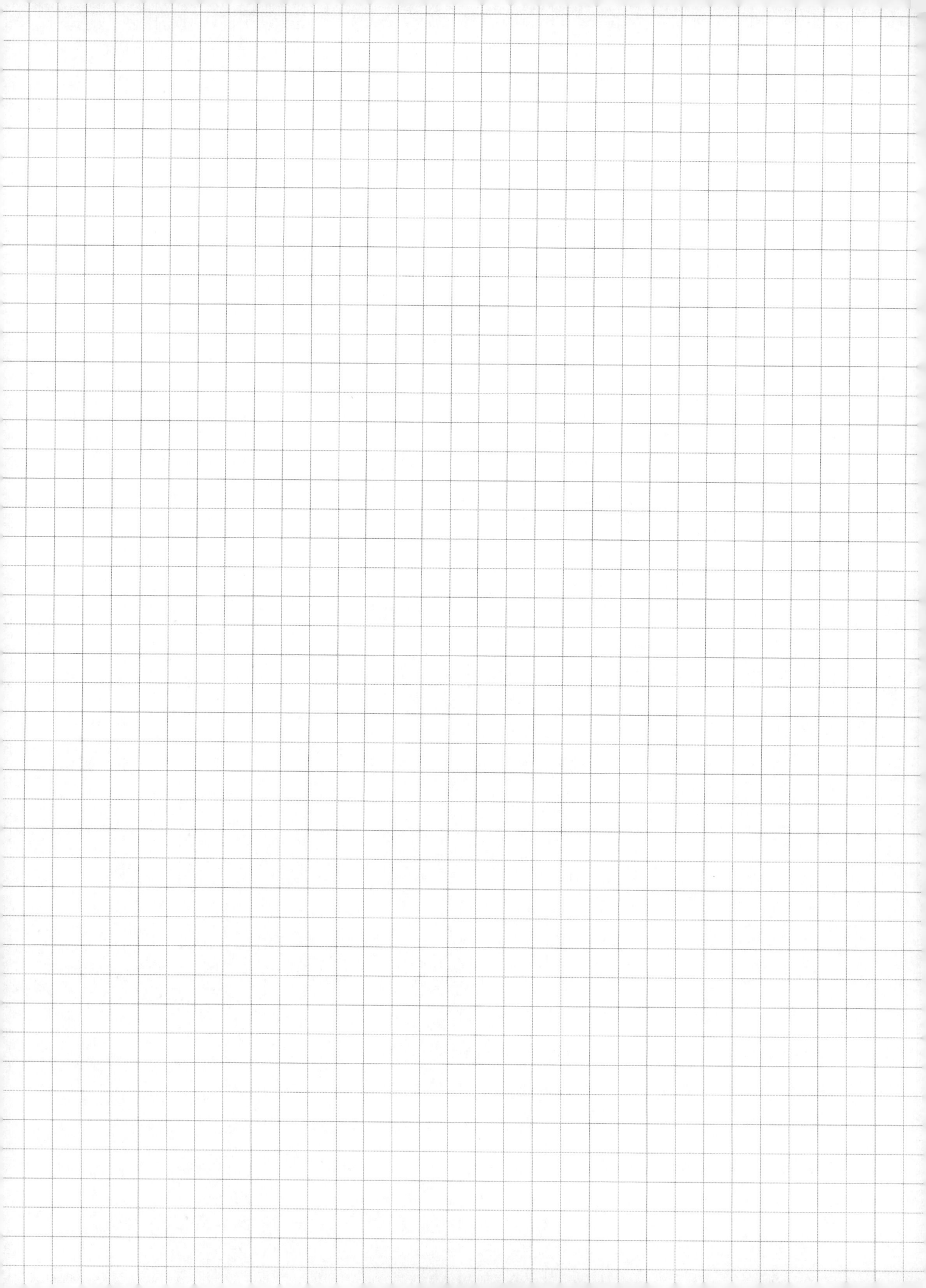

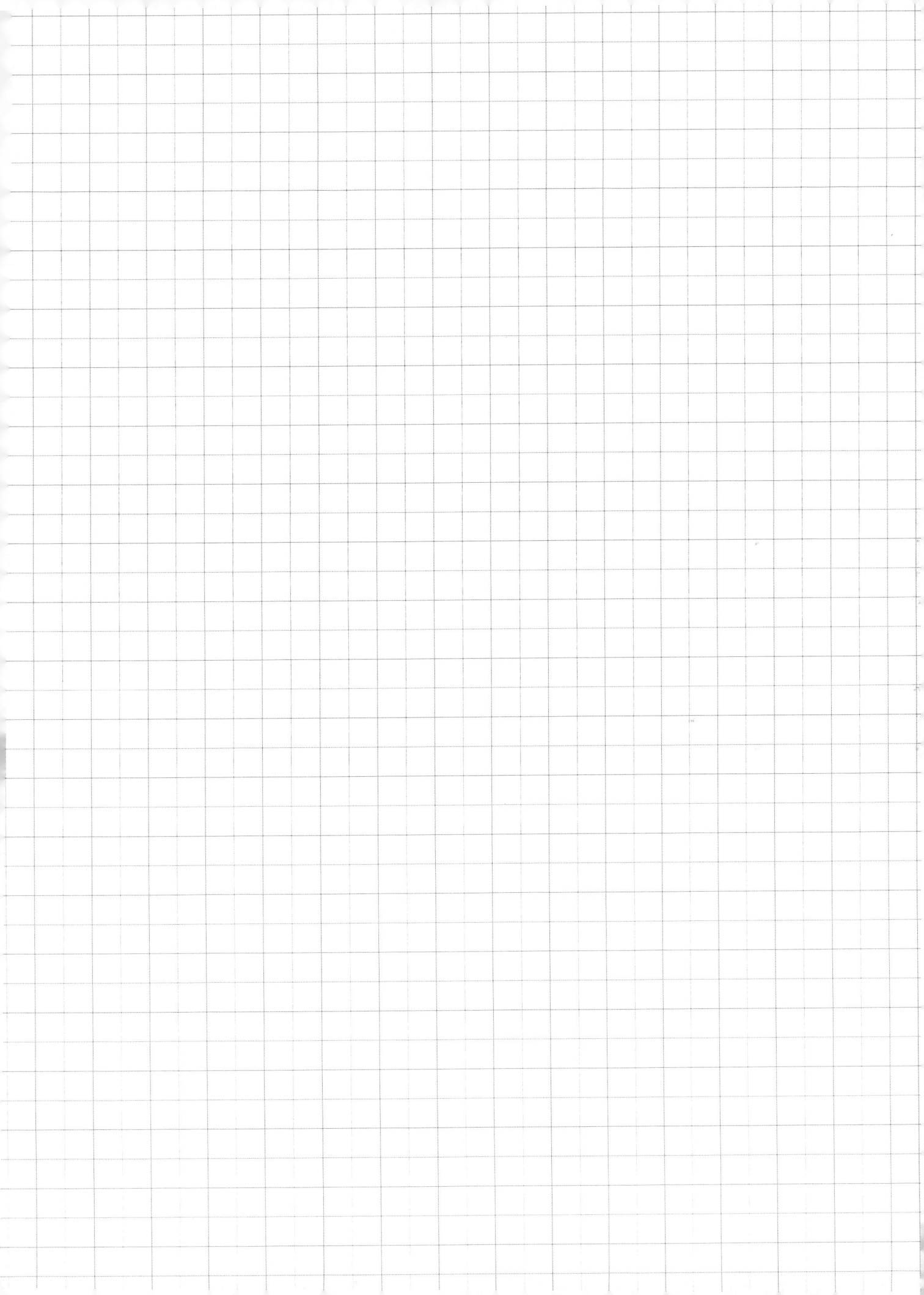

Made in the USA
Middletown, DE
31 August 2024

60110071R00113